D0411390

1097.

NORTH JUNIOR

- 5 FEB 1998   1 6 JUN 2000   2 9 JAN 2005

- 2 MAR 1998

1 9 NOV 1998   1 9 SEP 2000 2 9 SEP 2006
                - 5 APR 2001   2 3 APR 2009

2 3 JAN 1999

                1 6 FEB 2004   3 0 JUL 2011

1 5 MAR 1999
        1 1 OCT 1999   1 7 JUL 2004
                                        2 5 SEP 2011
                                        2 7 NOV 2011
                1 5 MAR 2007

Lib.1

"It wasn't me!"
LEARNING ABOUT HONESTY
Brian Moses and Mike Gordon

WAYLAND

The VALUES series:

"EXCUSE ME" LEARNING ABOUT **POLITENESS**
"I DON'T CARE!" LEARNING ABOUT **RESPECT**
"I'LL DO IT!" TAKING **RESPONSIBILITY**
"IT WASN'T ME!" LEARNING ABOUT **HONESTY**

Editor: Sarah Doughty
Designer: Malcolm Walker

First published in 1997 by
Wayland Publishers Ltd
61 Western Road, Hove
East Sussex BN3 1JD

Find Wayland on the internet at http://www.wayland.co.uk

British Library Cataloguing in Publication Data
"It wasn't me" : learning about honesty. – (Values)
1. Honesty – Juvenile literature 2. Truthfulness and
falsehood – Juvenile literature
I. Title II. Gordon, Mike, 1948 –
177.3

ISBN 0 7502 2092 9

Printed and bound by G. Canale & C.S.p.A.,
Turin

CONTENTS

How honest are you? When did you last own up to something you did wrong? Was it:

yesterday?

last week?

last year ... ?

... NEVER?

So who did you blame?
Was it:

your sister?

the baby?

the dog?

If you always try to be honest,
everyone will trust you:

your parents

your friends

You can look after it.

your teachers

I know I can trust you.

7

But if you are dishonest and tell lies,
it can lead to all sorts of trouble –

9

A lie can grow and grow ...

like a snowball rolling
down a mountainside.

A lie can quickly spread ...

like ink spilt on a table cloth.

It can follow you around ...

like a dog barking at
your heels ...

like a buzzing fly that won't leave you alone.

Sometimes we tell lies to impress our friends .,.

I'm going to Disneyland!

But if we do tell lies and we are found out, we will look rather silly.

17

Sometimes we tell lies to avoid
something we don't like doing.

But usually we get found out.

I think you must be a magician. I bought a new tube of toothpaste and it hasn't left the box!

Sometimes grown-ups are not as truthful as they could be.

Sometimes we do tell white lies so that we don't hurt other people's feelings.

Thank you so much for the present, it's just the kind of thing I like.

Accidents sometimes
happen ...

24

It takes courage to be honest and own up that you did something wrong.

You're blaming the wrong person. I broke the window.

25

When your friends tell lies
and get you into trouble,
you feel angry.

You don't want to
speak to them.

But remember what happens when you tell a lie.

Your mum and dad might be cross, but they forgive you.

And it's good to forgive your friends too.

If there was a competition for telling the truth, would you win First Prize?

Would you receive a silver cup for being champion truth teller?

And would you keep on
winning it?

NOTES FOR PARENTS AND TEACHERS

Read the books with children either individually or in groups, then ask them the questions on pages 4/5. Talk about the answers they give you – are they being totally honest? What do they feel about the ways in which lies are pictured on pages 10/11 and 12/13? Can they think of other ideas for showing how lies can grow and spread? Some children might like to illustrate their ideas.

Point out to the children that everyone is guilty of telling lies occasionally, but can it ever be right to tell lies? Ask the children if anyone has ever lied to them. How did they feel at the time? Perhaps a personal experience of a lie could be used to inspire a story. This could be written as a simple narrative or as a picture story which could be read to younger children. Perhaps the lie in the story could grow and spread causing all kinds of trouble ...

I told a lie to my mum. She believed me and she went round to Jason's house and repeated the lie to his parents. They were very upset and went to school to see my teacher. They repeated the lie to him. He repeated it to my head teacher. And that's why I'm standing here in his room while he telephones my mum and tells her my lie once again.

Sometimes it is easier to tell a lie than to tell the truth. Have the children heard the saying, 'honesty is the best policy'? What does this mean? Sometimes it takes great courage to tell the truth. Read children the story of George Washington cutting down the cherry tree. Sometimes telling a lie can lead to dreadful consequences. Tell the stories of 'Matilda' by Hillaire Belloc and 'The Boy Who Cried Wolf' from Aesop's Fables. Can children re-write these stories in their own words?

There are occasions where the deliberate telling of lies (or big fibs!) can be fun. Suggest that children write five lies about a subject – their dog, cat, family car, the sun, the sea, maths lessons, etc. These can help us see something from a different point of view, and after all, many of our poets' best images are lies! Also try making up statements that are either true or false. (The Guinness Book of Records is useful for finding out odd facts.) Test these out on children; e.g. elephants can't jump ... true or false? (Answer – true)

These ideas will satisfy a number of Attainment Targets in the National Curriculum at Key Stage 1.

BOOKS TO READ

'Matilda' by Hillaire Belloc (OUP, 1995)
A cautionary tale. Can be found in *'The New Oxford Treasury of Children's Poems'* edited by Michael Harrison & Christopher Stuart-Clark.

'The Best of Aesop's Fables' retold by Margaret Clark (Walker Books, 1990)
Contains *'The Boy Who Cried Wolf'* – a cautionary tale about a boy who tells the same lie too many times.

'Pinocchio' (several versions available)
Every time Pinocchio tells a lie his nose grows longer.

'Dilly Tells the Truth' by Tony Bradman (Mammoth)
Dilly the Dinosaur is always getting into trouble for not telling the truth but on the day when he is totally honest he gets into trouble again.

'On The Way Home' by Jill Murphy (Macmillan, 1982)
On the way home with a grazed knee Claire tells a lot of fibs about how it happened. In the end we discover the truth.

'The Fib and Other Stories' by George Layton (Collins Lions, 1981)
Title story *'The Fib'* could raise a number of questions about the ethics of telling white lies. (For the older end of the age range.)

INDEX